ANIMAL PARTS

EARS

Elizabeth Miles

Heinemann Library
Chicago, Illinois

© 2003 Reed Educational & Professional Publishing
Published by Heinemann Library,
an imprint of Reed Educational & Professional Publishing,
Chicago, Illinois

Customer Service 888-454-2279

Visit our website at www.heinemannlibrary.com

Designed by David Oakley at Arnos Design
Originated by Ambassador Litho Ltd
Printed in Hong Kong

07 06 05 04 03
10 9 8 7 6 5 4 3 2 1

Library of Congress Cataloging-in-Publication Data
Miles, Elizabeth, 1960-
 Ears / Elizabeth Miles.
   p. cm. -- (Animal parts)
Summary: Briefly describes how the ears of various animals differ in
size, placement, and function.
 ISBN 1-40340-014-8 (HC), 1-40340-423-2 (Pbk)
 1. Ear--Juvenile literature. [1. Ear.] I. Title. II. Series: Miles, Elizabeth, 1960-   . Animal parts.
 QL948 .M56 2002
 573.8'9--dc21
                          2001006752

Acknowledgments
The author and publishers are grateful to the following for permission to reproduce copyright material: p. 4, Photodisc; p. 5, OSF/Mark Hamblin; pp. 6, 26, Bruce Coleman Collection/Hans Reinhard; p. 7, Bruce Coleman Collection/Staffan Widstrand; p. 8, BBC NHU/David Welling; p. 9, NHPA/Anthony Bannister; p. 10, NHPA/Morten Strange; p. 11, Bruce Coleman Collection/Robert Maier; p. 12, Bruce Coleman Collection/Dr Eckart Pott; p. 13, BBC NHU/Peter Blackwell; p. 14, Bruce Coleman Collection/Pacific Stock; p. 15, OSF/Root Okapia; p. 16, Digital Stock; pp. 17, 30, digital vision; p. 18, OSF/Paul McCullagh; p. 19, BBC NHU/Torsten Brehm; pp. 20, 27, Corbis; p. 21, BBC NHU/Anup Shah; p. 22, Corbis/Charles Philip; p. 23, BBC NHU/Ingo Arndt; p. 24, Bruce Coleman Collection/Kim Taylor; p. 25, OSF/Konrad Wothe; p. 28, BBC NHU/Pete Oxford; p. 29, Bruce Coleman Collection/John Cancalosi.

Cover photograph reproduced with permission of NHPA.

Every effort has been made to contact copyright holders of any material reproduced in this book. Any omissions will be rectified in subsequent printings if notice is given to the publisher.

Some words are shown in bold, **like this.** You can find out what they mean by looking in the glossary.

Contents

Animals Have Ears

People and many other animals have ears. You use your ears to listen to all sorts of sounds. Hearing helps you to be aware of the world around you.

Animal ears are all different shapes and
sizes. Some rabbits have long, floppy ears.
Rabbits' ears look different from your ears.

Outer Ears

Many animals have ears that are easy to see. Some parts stick out. A donkey's **outer ears** collect sounds. The sounds then go into the donkey's **ear holes.**

Birds have no outer ears. They only have ear holes. This vulture has one ear hole on each side of its head. Sounds go into the holes so the bird can hear them.

Pointed Ears

The lynx has pointed ears shaped like **triangles.** Tufts of hair grow from the tips. The tufts help the lynx to hear when it is hunting in the long grass.

Aardvarks' ears are long and pointed
to help them hear. These animals are
nocturnal. They spend the night hunting
for **insects** to eat. They can hear the
sounds of **termites** in a nest.

Rounded Ears

The slow loris has rounded ears that gather sounds from the forest. The loris uses its **sense** of hearing and of smell to search for birds and **insects** to eat.

Mice use their rounded ears to hear each other's squeaks. Baby mice squeak to their mother. The mother mouse listens to make sure they are safe.

Big Ears

African elephants have the biggest ears of any **mammal.** They use them to listen to the calls of other elephants. They flap their ears to keep cool, too.

At night, foxes use their ears to hunt for food in the dark. A bat-eared fox has big, **sensitive** ears. Its sharp hearing helps it to find **insects** to eat.

Small Ears

Sea lions live and hunt in the sea. Their tiny ears do not stick out and slow them down when they swim. You can barely see their small **outer ears.**

A hippopotamus has tiny ears that it can close. To keep cool, hippopotamuses spend lots of time in rivers and lakes. They close their ears to stop water from getting in.

Hidden Ears

Birds' ears are often hidden by feathers. A bird has an **ear hole** on each side of its head. Kingfishers like this one listen to each other's songs and calls.

A snake's ears are completely hidden. It does not have ear holes. Because a snake cannot hear well, it depends on its other **senses,** such as sight and smell.

Ears on Top

Many animals have ears on the top of their heads. When zebras are busy drinking or **grazing,** their ears help them listen for danger.

A hare has tall ears on the top of its head.
It sits very still with its ears sticking up above
the grass. If it hears a **predator** coming, it
quickly runs away.

Ears on the Sides

Monkeys and apes have ears on the sides of their heads. Howler monkeys often listen to each other calling. They shout to other **troops** so that they keep away.

African buffalo have ears that stick out on the sides. Huge curved horns stand out above their ears. If a buffalo hears a lion, it may chase it away with its sharp horns.

Moving Ears

Many animals raise their **outer ears** when they listen. It helps them to hear better. Sheep dogs do this when they listen to orders from the **shepherd.**

Many animals, such as kangaroos, can turn each ear in a different direction. This helps them learn which direction a sound is coming from.

Ears in the Dark

Many **nocturnal** animals use their ears to find **prey** in the dark. The long-eared bat's ears help it find moths to eat. It listens for **echoes** to find its way.

Kiwis are nocturnal birds that cannot fly.
They cannot see each other well at night,
so they use their ears to listen for each
other's calls.

Underwater Ears

You cannot see fishes' ears. They are hidden inside their heads. They can hear well in the water. Catfish hear so well that they can hear noises made on shore.

Trout hear very well. If a trout hears a
predator getting into the water, it swims
away to safety.

Ears on Legs!

Some **insects** have ears in strange places. Crickets have ears on their front legs. They use their ears to listen for other crickets.

Instead of ears, a spider uses hairs to pick up sounds. Rows of special hairs on its legs pick up **vibrations.** These tell the spider if a moving animal is large or small. If it is large, the spider might hide.

Fact File

🐺 Dogs' ears can hear sounds that people cannot hear. They can hear very high sounds, like the sounds of a whistle.

🐺 A bird living in a large group can hear the sound of its own chick, even among all the other singing birds and chicks.

🐺 Crocodiles have ears on the tops of their heads. They can lie in the water with their ears sticking out. This means they can hear while they are hiding.

Eastern gray kangaroos have a good sense of hearing.

Glossary

ear hole   part of an ear into which sound travels

echo   sound, such as a shout, that comes back through the air

graze   eat low-growing grass or plants

insect   small animal with three main parts to its body and six legs

mammal   animal that feeds its babies with the mother's milk. People are mammals.

nocturnal   awake and active at night, not during the day

outer ear   part of the ear that sticks out from the head

predator   animal that hunts other animals for food

prey   animals hunted as food

sense   way of being aware of the world (seeing, hearing, smelling, touching, and tasting are senses)

sensitive   pick up sounds easily

shepherd   person who looks after sheep

termite   insect that lives in a very large group

triangle   shape with three corners

troop   group of monkeys

vibration   tiny movement made by sounds

More Books to Read

Miles, Elizabeth. *Eyes*. Chicago: Heinemann Library, 2003.

Miles, Elizabeth. *Legs and Feet*. Chicago: Heinemann Library, 2003.

Miles, Elizabeth. *Mouths and Teeth*. Chicago: Heinemann Library, 2003.

Miles, Elizabeth. *Noses*. Chicago: Heinemann Library, 2003.

Miles, Elizabeth. *Paws and Claws*. Chicago: Heinemann Library, 2003.

Miles, Elizabeth. *Tails*. Chicago: Heinemann Library, 2003.

Index